THE ANTI-POPULIST MANIFESTO

A Survival Guide for the West

I0407713

Contents

THE ANTI-POPULIST MANIFESTO

A Survival Guide for the West

FOREWORD

Why this Guide will never be Followed

It seems that the mainstream liberal press in all western countries is bemoaning the rise of various populist parties/movements or individuals of the right. Public opinion polling reveals that support for such candidates is at record levels. Indeed, the actual results of elections have shown that parties and candidates offering so-called 'populist' programs – if not successful – enjoy previously unheard-of levels of support.

A short list includes the election of Donald Trump as President of the United States, the 'Brexit' vote in the United Kingdom, the near-election of a far right wing candidate for Austria's president, the support for the National Front in France, Geert Wilders' Freedom Party in the Netherlands, the 5 Star Movement in Italy, the election of right wing governments in Poland and Hungary, the surge of the True Finns in Finland. The list could go on.

The mainstream press notes the drift away from 'traditional' mainstream parties and the increasing splintering of the vote among newer, smaller parties offering simplistic solutions to seemingly intractable problems. 'Globalisation' is usually held to blame. The mainstream parties are at a loss to answer the economic and social demands of the majority of their people. The attraction of the populists is that they do profess to have answers. The fact that those answers are more often than not spurious, short-term and mostly ineffective does not detract from their appeal. As Mr Trump asserted on many occasions during his campaign, "What have you got to lose".

Mainstream political parties these days are either centre-right or centre-left. There is little difference between the two: the former unashamedly 'pro-business' and bugger the poor, while the latter is but a paler version offering only to ameliorate the excesses of rampant capitalism on those at the bottom of the pile. Both are slaves to the corporate world – particularly large corporations that transcend national boundaries. No wonder there is a drift away from the mainstream parties: the old left-right spectrum does not apply any longer. People's views are more complicated than the old system allows.

This manifesto has a few underlying assumptions or beliefs. If you do not share these beliefs, you will reject the remedies set out in the pages that follow. Those fundamental rules are:

1. The role of the State is two-fold:

    (i)   to protect its citizens and residents; and

    (ii)   to advance the interests of the people.

2. Everyone (and I mean everyone) has the primary responsibility to support themselves and their minor children.

3. Everyone is responsible for their actions.

You may think that these few rules are okay. They certainly seem innocuous enough. But most people have not followed each rule through to its logical conclusion. When presented with the practical consequences of following through with such simple formulae, I suspect that most people will recoil.

I suspect that most people do not want to pay the price; after all, they didn't cause the problem. Let someone else do the heavy lifting. Or, if only those foreigners were stopped coming into the country, the rest of us, the real people anyway, would be better off. Unfortunately, the solutions to the problems of the West, and its ultimate survival, demand that all play a part in the repair process.

What does 'protect its people and residents' mean?

This is probably the simplest of the basic rules set out above. It simply means that the State must safeguard the external borders of the nation from foreign threats and invasion. This means threats from both other nations and groups as well as individuals.

The world order is based on nation-states, whether you like it or not. Whilst that remains the situation, the State has a responsibility for strong and effective national defence and a rigorous and uncompromising border-protection function. The left has gone soft in these areas and has bled support as a result.

Security also involves internal security, or traditional policing. Policing must be consistent with the values of a free and democratic liberal society (we are talking about a survival guide for the West after all). To this end, the State must ensure that the values of liberal-democracy are shared by its people. The writer has yet to come across any more palatable model of government for a large group of people than parliamentary democracy (for further reading, I recommend Robert A Dahl's 'After the Revolution?').

Advancing the Interests of the People

Put simply, the State must strive to achieve the maximum amount of economic well-being for the maximum amount of its citizens (this includes lawful residents from here on). But it doesn't end with money. The State must provide a system of affordable health care and also provide a system of education that ensures that every person has an equal opportunity to realize their fullest potential.

An advanced state needs advanced infrastructure and livable cities.

Of course, everything depends on the environment. The obligation of the State to protect its people extends to more than national defence. The State must safeguard, preserve and remedy the very land itself.

Personal Responsibility

Such a simple notion. Everyone agrees with it. Right?

You support yourself and your family.

You make a decision, your bear the consequences.

It's all so easy.

But a corporation is a legal person. What about when a corporation makes a decision. Well, of course, the corporation is responsible. All of us, I am sure, have experienced the phenomenon of dealing with a large corporation and being aggrieved by a decision or action it has made/taken. But a corporation acts through individuals. A corporation has a Board of Directors and/or managers. When the corporation gets it wrong we find that no one is responsible, no one is to blame. No individual is accountable. And the financial resources available to large corporations these days often exceeds that available to small nations. What hope does an aggrieved citizen have of fair redress? A penalty that is imposed for corporate malfeasance is more often than not a drop in the ocean. There is, in effect, no responsibility for corporate wrongdoing. The decision-maker, if identified, usually doesn't pay. The senior managers certainly don't pay the price in a direct sense. If anyone pays, it is the shareholder: the most remote of corporate members. Nothing changes because the guilty decision-maker and management are not held publicly accountable.

You receive social security benefits. You say you have an entitlement to benefits from the State. But the government gets its income from taxing others. What right do you have in asking the government to put its hand in my pocket, take my money, and give it to you? The safety net has, for far too many people, become a right of entitlement.

The Role of the Media

Most mainstream media publishers are corporations, and large ones at that. It is precisely these corporations that this manifesto lays the blame for much that is wrong in modern Western liberal-democratic society. So, I do not expect that this document will be well received in the mainstream public media. If it does achieve some prominence, I expect that it – and its author – to be mercilessly and viciously attacked.

I have always found it useful – when searching for the identity of the owner of any action – to ask the simple question, 'Who profits'. The answer invariably points us in the right direction.

A Lost Cause

The solution to the problems of the West requires collective action. Everyone must contribute. But in societies where just about everyone has their 'snout in the trough' of government concessions, where success depends on governments taking back and citizens (including corporate citizens) contributing more, the solution is impossible to achieve. Do you think that the solutions are painless? Or only that someone else should pay the price?

The examples given in this Manifesto are from the experience of Australia. But the sorts of policies discussed are akin to all western liberal-democracies. Citizens of the West are confronted with a choice between, on the one hand, social wealth with reasonable private wealth, and, on the other, unfettered individual wealth. The distribution of wealth in Western societies is scandalous, with the top few owning more than the bottom half. I maintain that that situation is simply not sustainable.

Many readers may well think this book has some good ideas, but dislike the rest. The problem with cherry-picking only some plans is that the traditional parties will pick only watered down versions of those it likes and leave everything else unchanged. Make no mistake, the problems of the West require radical surgery if the patient is to be saved. It is because we believe that not enough people have the stomach for it or simply have too much money and/or power to lose that we have come to believe that this blueprint is doomed to be ignored.

That means that the patient will die.

Chapter 1 - Taxation

"Taxation buys civilization"

Oliver Wendell Holmes

"In ninety-nine cases out of hundred, the answer to the question, 'Why?' is, 'Money.'"

How does a government defend the nation and advance the interests of its people? With money of course. And where does a government get its money from? You are a genius: yes, taxation.

Almost every western country has a budget deficit. For many it is at dangerous levels. Some, like Greece, have tipped over the edge. All States cite the need for 'budget repair' but none have the stomach to do what is required. For the conservative parties, budget repair is code for reducing social benefits that will impact the poorest members of the community while enhancing the benefits available to the wealthy and big business. For the social democrats, up taxes on the rich a bit but leave the unsustainable level of government spending largely untouched. Mainstream parties by and large address only one (and opposite) side of the problem, and even then in a half-hearted manner. No wonder nothing gets solved. This exemplifies the problem of cherry-picking adverted to earlier. Mainstream parties aim to protect their political support base, while simultaneously see that support base being eroded. They are powerless to act.

They are not the solution, but are part of the problem. No wonder people are turning away from them in droves.

A Simplified Tax System.

Australian Taxation law comprises thousands of pages and is set out in multiple pieces of legislation. It is incredibly complex. Complexity begets litigation: cases take up an extraordinary amount of court resources (for the rich and powerful, of course: ordinary people simply do not have the resources to challenge taxation rulings).

Taxation law is amended to cover every new means of avoidance and evasion that the best legal minds have so far devised. New schemes, it seems, are promoted on a consistent basis. The legislation has become immensely complex and cumbersome. Yet despite the efforts of governments, the largest corporations manage to – legally – pay only miniscule proportions of their income in tax. There have been international meetings and conventions by governments in their efforts to grapple with this problem. They commonly say that it is an international problem that requires a coordinated international response. And nothing gets done.

What a load of codswallop!

Income taxes are really taxes on gross profit (or 'taxable income'), not income or revenue. Gross profit or taxable income is the amount left after various deductions are made, for example, operating expenses and work expenses.

Multi-national corporations can reduce their tax by inflating the purchase price of the products that they buy from an overseas supplier that happens to be themselves in another name. Their overseas company is set up in a low tax country.

Try these figures out for size: in the 2014-2015 financial year, Google had a total income in Australia of A$438,687,915. Its 'taxable income' was A$106,097,095 yet the corporation paid only A$12,171,091 in company tax to the government of Australia. That represents a tax of 3% of its total income and 11% of its so-called 'taxable income' (Source: Australian Taxation Office).

During the same year, Nissan Motor Co Australia Pty Ltd had a total income of A$2,452,404,125 (that's over 2.4 billion Australian dollars) and yet had a company tax liability of $476!

And the major parties in Australia are calling for a lowering of the company tax rate (currently 30%) that none, it seems, appear to pay anyway.

Policy 1 – A revenue tax of 20%

All trading enterprises will pay a flat tax rate of 20% of their total sales.

No deductions for expenses.

The current company tax to be abolished.

The tax would be paid on a monthly basis as GST presently is.

Using our Google example above, if this formula had been operating, Google would have paid tax to the people of Australia amounting to A$87,737,583 or more than seven times what it actually paid.

Or with Nissan, the government of Australia would have received A$490,480,824! That's a lot of schools and hospitals.

Using the same Australian Taxation Office source, DURING THE FINANCIAL YEAR 2014-2015, 670 LARGE COMPANIES PAID NO CORPORATE TAX.

According to Taxation Statistics published by the Australian Taxation Office, during the 2013-2014 financial year, companies in Australia had a total income from all sources of A$ 2,714,482,880,043. This number is so big I am not exactly sure what is. If we applied our 20% flat revenue tax to that figure, the government (and people) of Australia would have collected company tax in that year of A$ 542,896,576,008. I think that is 542.896 billion dollars.

So much for the budget deficit. Goodbye sovereign debt.

Policy 2 – Abolish the Personal Income Tax tax-free threshold

Every income earner must pay tax.

People on social security benefits must pay tax as it is their obligation as citizens.

Currently in Australia, the first $18,200 of your yearly income is not taxed. You can earn up to $20,542 (effective since the 2012/2013 financial year) before any personal income tax is payable, when taking into account the Low Income Tax Offset.

This tax-free threshold (as well as high marginal rates of taxation) is the reason why people engage in income-splitting. It also is the reason why for many social security dependent people, there is a financial disincentive to actually work for a living.

Policy 3 – Income/Revenue tax – a flat rate of 20% for all.

Simple. Whatever you earn, one-fifth goes to the State.

Together with the abolition of the tax-free threshold (see below), there would be no benefit in income-splitting or family trusts as a means of tax minimization.

Policy 4 – Abolish all tax deductions and offsets.

Tax is payable on total gross income. That's it. Nice and simple.

Policy 5 – Extend Expenditure Taxes (GST) to everything

No exceptions.

Policy 6 – Raise the Expenditure Tax (GST) rate

It must be at least 12½ %.

Policy 7 – End Income-Splitting

No more bogus family employees.

What is income splitting & How it works.

Say you have a single-income couple on $100,000pa and they are able to income split, they could distribute the $100,000 equally between them, so that their average tax rate is 17.1 per cent as a couple, compared to 26.9 per cent before the split.

If the couple has children or other family members, they could benefit further by distributing the income to them as well. For example, if they have two children over the age of 18, they can distribute $25,000 to each member of the family, and each pay tax of $1,293, or an average tax rate of 5.2 per cent.

Policy 8 – Abolish the law of Trusts

A legal mechanism front and centre used in tax minimization and avoidance. (works as an income-splitting mechanism).

Policy 8 – End Negative-Gearing

Logically follows from Policy 4.

Policy 9 – Abolish Taxation Exemptions and Concessions for Charities & Religious Institutions

Policy 10 – End all Subsidies, Rebates & Tax Offsets

This includes all:

- child-care rebates;

- rural diesel rebates;

- private health insurance rebates

- low income tax offsets

Policy 11- Remove all Superannuation Concessions

All superannuation contributions above the statutory minimum to come from after-tax income taxed at the applicable marginally rate of taxation (or 20% if our policy is adopted).

Policy 12 – End Franking of Dividends

Policy 13 – Taxation of Deceased Estates

Why should someone profit without effort?

The silver spoon must be withdrawn to some extent.

More of a level start for all must be strived for.

A progressive system should be introduced based on the gross value of an estate.

For example: 10% for estates under $5 million.

20% for estates between $5M and $10M

50% for estates between $10M and $20M

75% for estates above $20M.

Policy 14 – End Family Support Payments/Concessions

You support your family, not others'.

Policy 15 – Maintain & Extend 'Social Taxes'

- continue the high taxation of cigarettes and alcohol

- introduce a tax on sugar

- introduce a tax on bottles/containers to encourage recycling.

Policy 16 - Superannuation Guarantee Levy

This superannuation guarantee levy must be increased to 20%.

This is an amount approaching that necessary to achieve economic independence at the end of a working life. If we are ever to wean ourselves off the weight of an ever increasing aged pension in a society that is ageing rapidly, decisive measures must be taken now.

Policy 17 – Superannuation Investment Fund.

- no superannuation fund will be permitted to charge an individual member more than a modest fixed amount for managing the investment.

- Where a fund's investment decisions result in a return on investment of less than the average fixed term deposit rate available with the leading four banks during a defined year, then that fund will be prohibited from charging any fees for that defined year.

- The state is to establish a superannuation investment fund subject to the same rules as outlined above. People will then have a further choice of fund administrator.

Policy 18 – Employers to be personally liable for non-payment of Levy

Any employer - that shall include its Directors, and senior managers and their partners and any other person or entity who has received a non-commercial financial benefit from that employer – found not to have made the superannuation levy payments required by law, shall be personally liable to make up the payments not made plus interest at the average fixed term deposit rate available with the leading four banks during the period of non payment.

Any such employer, including its Directors and senior managers, shall, in addition, be liable to criminal prosecution for the new criminal offence of failing to make the required payments and liable to imprisonment and banning from having any part in the ownership or management of any trading enterprise.

Policy 19 – Capital Gains Tax

All concessions to capital gains tax to be removed.

End of the exclusion of assets acquired prior to the commencement of the capital gains tax.

The tax payable will assessed on the gross capital gain at the taxpayer's highest marginal rate (or 20% if our policy above is adopted).

Capital gains Tax to be extended to include the family home.

Policy 20 – A Resource Rent Tax

Such taxes exist in various forms and at various rates in many nations and are 'charging arrangements imposed on non-renewable resources' (see recommendation 45 of the Henry Tax Review: 'Australia's Future Tax System').

It should be fixed at a rate of 25% of gross income. No deductions, no offsets, no exemptions.

Policy 21 – A Land Tax

This recommendation is taken from the Henry Tax Review: Recommendations 51 – 53. All private land should be prima facie subject to tax, but the rate of taxation can vary from zero upwards, depending on the per square metre value of the land.

Thus, low value land – such as agricultural holdings – could be taxed at zero, whilst higher value land would be taxed at a higher, progressive rate.

Policy 22 – Abolish Conveyancing Stamp Duty.

Stamp duty is a substantial tax on the transfer of real estate, especially burdening first time family home buyers.

For example, stamp duty on the purchase of a property with a value of $850,000 in the State of New South Wales (which is modest for Sydney) amounts to $33,740.

Policy 23 – Abolish Pay-roll Tax

A tax on employment? You're kidding.

Policy 24 – Road Transport Tax

'On routes where road freight is in direct competition with rail....heavy vehicles should face an additional charge...' (taken from Recommendation 64 of the Henry Tax Review, although this is not the recommendation as stated therein).

There are currently 8 types of benefit a person can receive from the Commonwealth Government, including Unemployment Benefit, Disability Support Pension, Aged Pension, Carers' Allowance. A print-out of the list of payments and services provided by the Australian Department of Human Services list a total of 139 separate payments, pensions, allowances, benefits, rebates, bonuses, supplements, scholarships, assistances and other services and programs.

Ending the age of Entitlement

There are – out of an adult population of 15 million people – 8 million people who receive some sort of social security benefit in Australia.

There are approximately 11.99 million people in Australia who are employed (many only part time or casual).

Accordingly, about 12 million people contribute to the financial support of approximately 8 million. With an ageing population and a declining birth-rate, how sustainable is that level of social security assistance?

As indicated earlier, it is the responsibility of each person to support himself and his/her family. That is, there is an obligation to earn your living and pay your own way. No coasting in life. No dipping in someone else's pockets for support. No taking someone else's hard-earned cash. In short, no bludging.

It is amazing to the author just how pervasive this sense of entitlement to a pension is. Older people typically say, "I've worked all my life and paid my taxes, now it's my turn to get something back."

Wrong!

You work to support yourself and your family.

You paid taxes because it was your obligation to society to do so.

You did not pay your taxes with a view to getting anything back from the State.

Your obligation to support yourself never ceases.

Policy 25 – Abolish all Pensions except the Unemployment Benefit

This reinforces the policy obligation that- prima facie - all must work to live.

Realistically, many people cannot work, and for them the social security safety net is still available.

Duties in caring for someone else is not an acceptable reason for not working. It is your responsibility to care for family.

A properly funded State care system will obviate the need to do so in any case.

Disability to be assessed by government doctors with a high threshold applicable.

Policy 26 - All pensions/benefits to be means-tested

Social security is meant to be a safety net to be accessed at last resort. An individual is expected to use his/her own resources to support themselves and their family before any recourse can be made to the State (that is, other people's money).

Why should someone else (perhaps a struggling worker with a family saving for their own home) contribute to the support of another person who owns a property worth millions?

It's so unfair as to be almost insane.

And yet this is exactly what happens in Australia.

It follows then that:

Policy 27 – No assets excluded from the means test

Policy 28 – Benefits Card

All social security benefits are to be accessed by a debit-type card.

The card could not be used for the purchase of cigarettes, alcohol or gambling or redeemed for cash.

Chapter 3 - Education

There is clearly a role for the State in ensuring that the values of a humanistic liberal-democracy are passed onto its citizens. We should not shy away from the fact that such 'socialisation' has always constituted a part of a modern education system and rightly so.

Yet we live in a society that is becoming more and more fractured. Where are our shared beliefs that form the basis of social harmony? Commonality of purpose has been undermined by the proliferation of a non-state education system. It is time for the State to step in and insist that the education of its citizens is too important to be left in the hands of non-state institutions.

Governments in Australia hand out billions of dollars for the benefit of private and religious schools/education. This could be better applied to a massive investment in and rejuvenation of the State educational system.

Policy 29 – End Non-Government Education

No money/concessions for private (including religious) education.

Compulsory acquisition (with fair compensation) of non-government educational assets.

Policy 30 – Prioritise Education

There must be a recognition of the primary importance of education to a well-functioning and orderly society. Education has always been the means of an individual achieving economic and social transformation. Education is the engine of social mobility and meeting economic and social aspirations.

Education is an end in itself.

Policy 31 – A system of Pre-School Education & Child-care

Just as the State currently insist that children commence formal schooling at say, age 5 or 6, and provides a system for doing so, it is proposed that a fully functioning and funded system of State schooling commence at a much earlier age, say at 3 years of age.

Children would be required to attend school every week day, but the hours of each days' attendance is to be modified with age.

A government-run system of child-care for children aged between 1 year of age and 3 years of age must be established. This would be staffed by appropriately qualified people and have a uniform curriculum. There would be no charge to the parent/s.

Policy 32 – Allow a younger school leaving age

Let's face it, not every person has the ability or the inclination to go to University.

Yet such students are compelled to attend school against their wishes and without any social benefit other than to keep them off the streets during the day.

What a waste of young lives.

What a cause of disruption to those other students who genuinely want to continue their schooling.

Some flexibility must be introduced into the educational system.

Thus, those children aged at least 16 years who are genuinely employed or engaged in technical or vocational studies are to be allowed to leave school.

Policy 33 – Return to a Genuine Apprenticeship System

The old system was, by and large, a better system of training tradespeople.

There must be a return to the one employer based system.

Policy 34 – No Apprentices – No Government Work

There is said to be a shortage of suitably qualified tradespeople in Australia. The years of neglecting and compromising the system of technical education is coming home to roost.

We must ensure that our society is producing the skilled people required by a modern properly functioning society.

One way is to mandate that any firm awarded a government contract must have a certain proportion of apprentices in the areas in which they operate. If not, no contract or termination of the contract with penalties.

Policy 35 – Free Tertiary Education

There should be no end to guaranteed and complete government educational funding at secondary school.

University and technical education must be completely free.

All young people who have the ability and inclination to continue their studies after high school should not be precluded by the cost.

It follows that the existing HECS scheme is to be abolished and all current debts under that scheme forgiven.

One of the most fundamental areas in which a state can protect and advance the well-being of its citizens is in the area of health. So, just as in the area of education policy, the State must prioritise the health system and invest heavily in this area.

Policy 36 – Maintain and extend Medicare

Medicare, under which every citizen is entitled to free health care in a public hospital, is the basis of the health system in Australia.

Whilst not being an expert in the area, the writer has spoken to many health professionals who maintain that it is the best system of public health in the western world. Medicare maintains a role for private medical practitioners whilst offering the universality that underpins fairness.

In Australia, quality health care is not the exclusive privilege of the rich, but the right of all.

There are gaps in the system, however.
One of these is:

Policy 37 – Extend Medicare to Dental Health

Policy 38 – Make Bulk-billing compulsory

No one should ever be out of pocket by going to the doctor.

Policy 39 – Massive investment in the Health System

The vast amounts of revenue generated from the adoption of the system of Taxation outlined in Chapter 1 will allow the level of investment in the health care system required to make the need for a private system of hospitals unnecessary.

Private Health Insurance is rightly regarded by most Australians as poor value for money. With a properly funded public health system, there would be no need for private health insurance. This would save the average family thousands of dollars each year.

There will no support of any kind to the private health system.

Where considered necessary, the State will compulsorily acquire – with fair compensation – private health assets.

Policy 40 – Abolish the Private Health Insurance Rebate

If an individual insists on having private health insurance, then they must be prepared to pay for it without any subsidy from other taxpayers.

Policy 41 – Maintain, Extend & Modify the Pharmaceutical Benefits Scheme

This system of state subsidies is another cornerstone of the best public health system in the western world. But again, it has room for improvement.

Firstly, new drugs must be brought under the schemes umbrella much more quickly.

The scheme must only be applicable to generically available drugs where such drugs are available.

There must be a requirement that all medical practitioners prescribe generic drugs where such drugs are available.

The price of any drug for sale in Australia must be no more than the lowest price of that drug available anywhere else in the world.

Health care professionals will be banned from accepting any gifts, benefits, payments or rewards of any nature from drug companies. There must be no compromise or corruption in the health system.

Policy 42 – Increase the Medicare levy to 5%

If you want the best, you must pay for it.

Policy 43 – A Mental Health Care System

Go to any local court house in the State of New South Wales. Sit in the list court. You will soon realize just how many of the people that appear before the courts charged with criminal offences have mental health issues. Ask legal-aid lawyers at the coal-face of our criminal justice system.

Our courts are often processing centres where mentally ill people are sent, not to mental health institutions, but to prison.

There was a time when mental health institutions did exist. But with the 1980's fetish for community-based care, the mental health hospitals were shut down and the valuable land on which they stood put up for sale.

Now the writer does not propose that every person with a mental health issue should be locked up in a mental hospital, but there are clearly individuals where that is the best course not only for them but for the community as a whole. Who pays the price for crimes committed by mentally-ill people? Their families, their victims.

Leave the criminal courts to deal with real criminals.

Shelter. Such a basic need. For many it has become an impossible dream to own their own home, be it apartment or house.

The author happens to believe that private ownership of accommodation is the best means of residence. People tend to look after what they own, take pride in it, preserve and enhance it. The author also believes – as is indicated above – that individuals have the responsibility of providing for themselves and their families.

The State can assist in achieving private ownership of housing in an affordable manner.

Policy 44 – State Construction/State Sale

The government, either directly or via private contractors, must build housing stock, both apartments and other medium density accommodation, as well as stand alone detached dwellings.

The government would then sell the accommodation to those in need without requiring a deposit.

The government would loan the purchase price to the purchaser, repayable weekly as a fixed proportion of income until the loan is repaid in full. The debt would be secured over the property as a mortgage as is currently the case with private lenders.

A nominal rate of interest equivalent to the rate of inflation would be charged.

Title to the property would be vested in the purchaser. Each person would be entitled to one only such loan/assistance.

The purchaser would be free to on-sell the property before the loan is discharged, but the debt (including interest) together with one half of the capital gain would be repayable to the government. Once the loan is completely repaid, the government would have no further involvement nor would it be entitled to one half of the capital gain.

Policy 45 – Developer Charges

These are currently levied by local and state governments but they should be at a level so that "they appropriately price infrastructure provided in housing developments" (recommendation 70: Henry Tax Review).

The age where the property developer reaps the profits leaving the rest of us to pay for infrastructure for the development must end.

Chapter 6 – Transport & Communications

Communications and transport infrastructure are vital to all citizens in a modern world, no matter whether they live in cities or outside. These assets impact tremendously on the quality of life of people in fundamental ways: from how much time we spend with our families, to access to the best in health care and education.

Policy 46 – a World Class Internet

Why must we settle for second best?

What is wrong with leading the world?

We can afford it, we simply need the vision and the will to do it.

Fibre to the home must be the norm.

The state must fund it. The costs will be recouped over time with affordable and reasonable internet access fees.

Policy 47 – Public Transport Must be Prioritised

This includes a world class road network.

Public transit systems must be modern, fast and affordable. Let's face it, rarely do they operate at a profit. But the savings made in pollution, congestion and time more than make up for the costs.

Publicly funded, no tolls.

The ever increasing cost of toll roads for city dwellers is becoming unsustainable and a real burden to the lower paid. The state must resume its responsibilities to finance and construct the public transport systems that are needed.

Chapter 7 – Foreign Investment, Primary Processing &

Corporate Governance

Policy 48 – Owning Residential Real Estate Banned

Regardless of the value, no foreign person is to be allowed to buy and/or own any residential real estate.

Policy 49 – At least 51% Locally owned.

All other property must be subject to a limit of 49% foreign owned/controlled.

Other countries have such limitations and their world has not collapsed. Majority local ownership ensures that businesses operating in Australia are amenable to government policy.

Policy 50 – Mandatory Pre-Export Primary Processing

Nations that export commodities unnecessarily export their jobs as well. There are few employment opportunities in digging up minerals, loading them onto a train and delivering them to a port and loading onto a bulk carrier. The price the nation receives for the unprocessed product is low by comparison with a processed product.

Our policy would ban the export of unprocessed products. Some value-added pre-export processing of the product must take place before being sent off.

An example in Australia is the export of live animals. How many times do we have to be confronted with sickening images of cruelty to our livestock at the hands of people in the country of destination? Well, there is a simple solution to that problem which is both employment-generating and value-adding. Namely, ban live exports of livestock and insist on slaughter (to acceptable 'humane' standards) within Australia prior to export.

But- you may ask - what if that is not acceptable to the customer? My answer is "Tough." You want our product, that is the condition. Otherwise, look elsewhere. The farmers are howling. I can here their whingeing (does it ever end?) in the middle of Sydney. Grow some balls! In a developing world, there will be no shortage of demand for premium agricultural products.

Policy 51 – Corporate Salaries

The level of salaries and bonuses paid to many corporation executives is simply obscene.

No employee of a corporation is to be paid (inclusive of all bonuses and any other payments whatsoever) more than 50 times the average income of the working population in the absence of a special resolution of the shareholders of that corporation requiring at least 75% of the voting rights of the company and, moreover, any such approval is subject to yearly review.

I simply do not accept the argument that people of sufficient quality cannot be found for an annual salary of 2 to 3 million dollars. In any case, it is open to the shareholders to pay more if they choose to do so.

Chapter 8 – Population Policy

Nearly every nation has a population policy of some sort. Australia has had a long-standing immigration program.

There appears to be some hysteria among mainstream politicians and the mainstream liberal media about the rights of a nation to determine just who is allowed to enter and reside in that nation. Surely it is the sovereign right of any country to make such determinations.

Immigration directly impacts the poorest of any community, simply because it is in those areas that new arrivals typically reside, for obvious reasons. Every wave of immigration has usually been associated with crime committed by elements of the new arrivals. Again, the victims of such crime tend to be the poor. When the poor cry out against immigration they are labeled bigots and racists by the chattering classes who are well insulated from the social costs of immigration.

Like all national policy, population policy must be determined on national self-interest, and not decided by others – domestic or otherwise – on the basis of what they happen to think is morally right.

A refugee is someone who is forced to leave their home and seek shelter in the first available place of refuge. A refugee is not someone who picks and chooses the place in which they would prefer to reside and then pay people smugglers big money to get them there. An economic migrant is not a refugee. A person who has the means to pay a people-smuggler is not a genuine refugee.

The cause of leaving will never be addressed if people simply take off and leave. Surely, they have the responsibility to effect the changes in their own countries that will remedy the problem. People often forget that the people of the West had to struggle and fight for the development of liberal democracy in their own countries.

More is to be gained by supporting refugees in the first country of refuge. By supplying support necessary to effect the changes required to solve the problem causing them to leave in the first place. By training and supplying them militarily in some cases. Let them fight for their freedom as our ancestors in the west had to fight and die for liberal democracy.

Immigration also has an environmental cost. It goes without saying that more people demand more resources that further strains the natural resources of a state.

Finally, immigration impacts on the employment prospects of unemployed citizens and the wage levels of those who are employed by creating a larger pool of unemployed people from which employers can draw creating a competition for jobs that impacts on the price of labour.

Policy 52 – No refugees to be Admitted

Policy 53 – Support to assist Refugees overseas.

Policy 54 – No special visas for foreign labour

Working holidays for young people excepted.

Policy 55 – Immigration to target compatible people

The priority of a government is to maintain, assist and advance its own citizens. That is nothing to be ashamed or embarrassed about. That means that the state should pick and choose only those immigrants whom it believes will be compatible with existing national values and who will not impose too much of a burden on the community and who will positively benefit the community.

We live in the real world. We have yet to see a successful multi-racial society.

People with intolerant views – including intolerant religious beliefs - should not be allowed to enter the country as immigrants. People who hold adherences above that of or incompatible with the values of liberal democracy must be excluded.

It is not wrong to discriminate. It is desirable to exercise discrimination for the benefit of the nation. If that means a ban on Muslim immigration, then so be it. If that means a ban on Chinese immigration, well that's ok. A nation has the right to determine its population mix and it does not have to be apologetic about it. If doing so brings criticism from any international body, including the UN, then

Australia should withdraw from the international convention on refugees and cease to fund any of its activities.

This is an area where the bleeding-heart left has lost its working class base. It is the working class – often the descendants of migrants themselves – who are at the social coal-face of immigration. They feel the consequences. Yet their heretofore leaders are championing the illegals, the queue-jumpers, the economic migrants, the sham and the real refugees over them. No wonder they are turning away from the parties of the centre and the left.

While there is significant unemployment or underemployment in the country, immigration should cease, simple.

Policy 56 – An end to Family Reunion

The sole criterion for immigration is the benefit to the nation not to any individual, family or group.

Policy 57 – Delayed Citizenship & Liability to Deportation

No migrant nor any member of that person's family should be permitted to become a citizen until their youngest child reaches the age of 18 years. Any non-citizen who commits a serious criminal offence – as well as their non-citizen family members – shall be deported to their country of origin.

It is your responsibility to raise your children to respect the laws and customs of your adoptive country. It's part of the compact between you and your new home. You break the compact, you go back. Simple.

Citizenship otherwise must only be available after 5 years' residence.

Chapter 9 – Energy and The Environment

These two areas are much intertwined.

Let's get one thing straight right off. The earth's climate is changing as a result of global warming. That much is indisputable. The debate – where there is any – centres around whether that global warming is as a result of, or contributed to by, human activity. The writer happens to believe that it is. Others will disagree. But consider this: if I am wrong, what are the consequences? The end of dirty industries and polluting activities together with the creation of whole new clean industry sectors of economic activity. Yes, many people employed in the old polluting industries will lose those jobs, but many new jobs will be created. Should past governments have banned the use of motor vehicles because blacksmiths would be put out of business? That is the way progress operates. And, oh, I might have to pay a few dollars more for my power.

But what if the opposing side of the argument is wrong? An increasing environmental catastrophe such as to threaten the very existence of hundreds of millions of human beings or even human existence itself.

What's the safest bet? It's a no-brainer.

Policy 58 – Renewable Energy

The aim is 100% renewable energy by 2030. It can be done. Don't believe the doomsayers, the coal industry or the politicians in the pockets of dirty industry.

The State must ban all new fossil-fuel energy generation.

The State must rapidly phase out and de-commission all existing fossil fuel power generation.

New renewable energy sources of power generation must be encouraged. That includes roof-top solar to industrial-scale solar, wind-energy, wave-energy, you name it.

The writer is open to nuclear power generation as a last resort, interim measure.

Policy 59 – An Emissions Trading Scheme

It's efficient. It's Cost-effective. It works.

Policy 60 – Environmental Crimes

Individuals, as well as corporations, must be held accountable for environmental damage.

The actual cost of both clean-up and environmental restitution must be paid for by the offenders.

Policy 61 – Mandating Worlds-Best Environmental Practices/Technology

The State must prescribe that the very best/cleanest practice and/or products are allowable.

Thus, only the best energy efficient cars can be sold/imported.

Only fuel that is equal to world's cleanest may be sold.

Industries that do not adopt world's best must incur penalties and, if still non-compliant, phased out.

Is this going to cost me?

Of course it is.

Chapter 10 -The Political Process

"He who pays the piper calls the tune."

One of the greatest threats to liberal-democracy in the modern era is the corruption of the political process by money. The lobbying industry is thriving. Politicians sell access to them by individuals and corporate representatives who want something from government. Do you think any business gives money to political parties and politicians without expecting something in return? What planet do you live on.

Our major political parties are beholden to the money-holders. Is it any wonder that the things that are necessary for social advancement never get done, or are so watered down as to be useless.

Policy 62 – No Political Donations
Full-Stop.

Policy 63 – A cap on spending by Parties & Politicians
This includes that sort of insidious indirect support that has become a feature of modern political campaigns, such as advertisements run by industry groups.

Policy 64 – A state-based system of election funding

Such a system operates already in Australia. This should be the only form of funding allowable.

Policy 65 – All 'lobbying' or approaches to government and all elected representatives must be in writing and be publicly released upon receipt.

Policy 66 – An Independent Commission Against Corruption

This must be established to ensure the fairness and integrity of the political process. A finding of corruption

Policy 67 – An Enforceable Register of Interests

What a joke the current Australian system is: 'Oh, I forgot to declare the 2 investment properties that I own.'

Any breach of the disclosure policy results in automatic disqualification from elected office, as would any finding of corrupt conduct, including breach of the funding and lobbying policies.

We must restore the people's confidence in the integrity of the electoral process. People must believe that their interests are less important to the man with money.

Policy 68 – Truth in Advertising

All advertising must be objectively truthful if presented as facts. If opinion or personal belief is being expressed, then that fact must be openly and clearly stated before the assertion of that opinion or belief.

Proof of objective truth must be made by an organization independent of the advertiser.

Policy 69 – A Case for Censorship?

A few years ago the writer would have been up in arms at such a proposition, but with the rise of the phenomenon of 'Alternative Facts', the abuse of the internet, then perhaps the time has come to look seriously at censorship or at least the application of the 'Truth in Advertising' Policy to the internet as well.

A related concern is on-line gambling. The writer is no wowser, but there are ample opportunities to gamble without the ease of on-line facilities.

Policy 70 – Open Government

All government discussion papers and commissioned reports as well as the terms of any proposed and finalised contracts must be available to the public and published on-line simultaneously with their release to the relevant minister/department.

The only exception is national security.

Policy 71- Compulsory Voting

It is the obligation of every citizen to vote as a minimum degree of participation in the democratic process.

Policy 72 – Proportional Representation

To ensure that all groups and opinions in society are reflected in the parliament. Also one of the best ways to ensure that the rights of minorities are heeded and protected.

The process encourages compromise and consensus rather than the dictates of the majority.

Chapter 11 – Commercial Honesty/State Enterprise

How sad that it is considered necessary to legislate for the simple requirement that people be honest when engaging in commercial transactions. The era of the con-man has reached its pinnacle. The 'shafting' of the other side is a cause of pride rather than shame.

Policy 73 – If you mislead the customer, you lose

Simple, you lie or trick someone else in a commercial transaction, then the other party can rescind the transaction and be restored to the position they would have been had not the transaction been entered into. In addition, the culprit is to be publicly names and be subject to both criminal and civil sanctions.

Policy 74 – State Enterprise in a Mixed Economy

Some of the greatest private enterprises in our society started out as government owned and operated institutions. In Australia, we have the Commonwealth Bank, Telstra (telecommunications), CSL (Commonwealth Serum Laboratories: drug developer and manufacturer), lotteries, betting agencies, ports, rail, various electricity and gas utilities. However, this country along with many others in the West embarked on a privatization frenzy: everything it seemed, was up for sale.

The experience has almost universally been one of higher costs and charges to the consumer. The Government gets a short term kick of funds that may or may not be used wisely, but foregoing, in the process, steady recurrent income and direct control and regulatory oversight over basic public services.

The calls for inquiries into the Banks, persistent concerns at price-gouging by oil companies, higher utility charges, to name a few are laughable. We all know that the companies will do whatever they can get away with in order to maximize profits and return to shareholders. We know that governments of the day - whose parties are in receipt of generous political donations – will make a verbal fuss but end up doing nothing.

Well, we live in a mixed economy, where the state is acknowledged to have a role to play along with private enterprise. Our economic system – we are told – thrives on competition. Well, let's give them a bit of competition.

In areas where there are real concerns regarding monopolistic or cartel behavior, or where basic public services are involved, the State should establish competing corporations in order to ensure fair pricing, restore trust and confidence, effective regulation as well as on-going return on investment to the budget bottom line.

Policy 75 – Corporate Managers/Directors Personally Liable

If a company does the wrong thing, the company pays. But the individuals within the corporation who made the relevant decision and whose duty it is to guide and direct the enterprise, are not held to account. This must change. What about when a company goes broke having not paid its employees' superannuation entitlements. Why should the state step in and pay? Those individuals responsible for ensuring that the payments were made should pay out of their own pockets.

All individuals directly involved in the particular wrong-doing as well as all Directors and senior managers of the corporation are to be directly and personally liable for that wrong-doing. That includes for civil and criminal penalties.

With power must come responsibility.

Well, you might ask, who would ever want to be a director or senior manager in those circumstances? I say, there will be hordes of able and ethical people who would be willing to take up the mantle.

Policy 76 – Presumption of Ownership of Assets

Of course, smart operators in the elite may seek to protect their assets from penalties by various means. Many of these schemes are subject to our taxation Policy above, but family assets are to be conclusively presumed to be at least 50% owned by each partner equally.

Chapter 12 – The Legal System

You think everyone is equal before the law?

If so, you obviously have little experience of our legal system.

How can an ordinary person take on a Bank or other large corporation? Those with money have access to the best legal resources available. They will wear you down, delay the process, threaten you with financial ruin if you lose, and even lie to the court and withhold evidence.

Our system of law is based on a contest between 2 equal adversaries. We know that that is not the reality. Money generally triumphs.

Policy 77 – Reform the Civil Law Process

This means abolishing the adversarial system in Civil Law (I can hear the howls of protest from the lawyers at the top end of town already).

Civil courts would be constituted by an independent judge/investigator who will hear from both sides.

Legal representation will be prohibited.

The rules of evidence will not apply.

Full-disclosure is required by all parties.

The hearing is to be conducted with little formality.

The role of the court is to actively investigate the claims of each party.

Decisions must be announced within 30 days of the commencement of proceedings.

There will be no orders for costs against party nor will security for costs be required.

Policy 78 – Compulsory Drug Treatment

Our courts have various drug treatment programs. However, they depend upon the willingness of the individual to apply for and accept treatment. This has got to end. The safety of the community should not be jeopardized by the wishes of a criminal. You break the law, and drugs are an issue: you do compulsory re-hab. Simple. And you stay there for as long as it takes for the treatment to be effective.

Of course, any program would contain other elements designed to prevent re-offending, such as real job training, psychological intervention and counseling where appropriate.

Policy 79 – Labour in Prison

There is no free ride in society, not even in prison. Prisoners must be put to work (when not training or under-going other rehabilitative programs) in productive enterprises that help to defray the costs of their incarceration.

Policy 80 – Restorative Justice

If you cause loss or damage, you are liable for its repair. If you have assets, these will be liquidated to pay the cost.

Chapter 13 – Aged Care

An ageing population is a feature of economic development. This is a mixed blessing as far as the economy is concerned. Aged people who are not financially independent call upon the State (that is, other citizens and taxpayers) for support. But as the proportion of non-working older people increases, there are relatively fewer people of working age to tax in order to meet the increasing burden.

It is for this reason that governments around the world have introduced schemes of mandatory retirement funding (superannuation in Australia) so that individuals assume more the responsibility for their own retirement support and there is, accordingly, less call on the resources of the State.

We have advocated some policies relating to Superannuation in Chapter 1.

Just as there are public hospitals, every citizen who needs it, will have a place in a properly resourced Aged Care facility, at heavily subsidized rates (or for no charge if the circumstances justify).

With an ageing population, this area of public policy is woefully inadequate, under-resourced and not given appropriate priority.

Senior citizens – like everyone else - deserve to be treated with respect and to have their various needs attended to with the highest quality. This area is for many people and families, a huge concern. Our care of the aged is, in far too many cases, a cause of shame.

Policy 81 – Abolish the Compulsory Retirement Age.

This follows from our policies set out in Chapter 2. The obligation to support yourself never ceases.

Policy 82 – Assist People to Live in their Homes

Many older people prefer to continue to live in their own home, but find it increasingly difficult to tend for themselves and maintain their homes.

The State should step in and provide home care assistance for these people.

There would a means-tested charge payable.

Policy 83 – A Properly Resourced System of State Retirement & Nursing Homes

For many people, the experience of the placing older family in a nursing home can be quite confronting. The quality of facilities is variable. The standard of care Can range from excellent to deplorable. Profit-run organisations will always be slaves to the bottom-line, and that means our older loved ones suffer.

Staff in such facilities can be questionable, in both training and character.

Older people and their families deserve the best care possible. They should not have to worry about proper care is being provided.

Accordingly, the State must establish a non-exclusive system of Aged Care so that high-quality affordable facilities are available to all who need them.

Policy 84 – Government Annuities

Recommendation 22 of the Henry Tax Review ('Australia's Future Tax System') provided that "the government should consider offering an immediate annuity and deferred annuity product that would allow a person to purchase a lifetime income."

We agree.

Chapter 14 - Expenditure Generally

This manifesto – if adopted – will see a huge amount of money flowing into government coffers. Money that could and should be used for the betterment of the people of the nation. But what irks ordinary taxpayers more than anything is to see their hard-earned taxes squandered and wasted by government on projects and organisations that are of dubious benefit to the citizenry generally or is directed towards advancing pet social ideas that should not be the province of government or, if it passes that test, is unnecessarily excessive.

I ask for only this: when any official – not matter how senior or junior - determines to spend taxpayers' money, that official should act as if the money were coming out of his/her pocket personally.

Afterword

Adopting the policies set out in this manifesto will not end globalization or impose a new protectionist order. The modern global economic structure has delivered huge benefits to people around the world. Economic development has raised millions – perhaps billions – of people out of poverty and given them hope for a better future for themselves and their children. Besides, I believe that it is irreversible.

I do not believe that globalization is the cause of the West's problems. Rather, it is the greed and abuse of power practiced by those who have profited the most. One would have thought that those very people who have gained the most and who have the most to lose, would do all they could to preserve and better the system, rather than contribute to its downfall.

And by the gutless and/or corrupt politicians in the pockets of the corporations and the rich who betray the interests of the very people who elected them and trusted them to look after the interests of the people.

www.ingramcontent.com/pod-product-compliance
Lightning Source LLC
Chambersburg PA
CBHW072117280526
45788CB00006B/2530